MW00774130

How to

Pass Your Patrol

and Other Tips for Earning the

Black & Gold

Explained by a U.S. Army Ranger Instructor

Background pattern for cover by Chris Spooner

http://blog.spoongraphics.co.uk/

Creatwal Publishing
ISBN-13: 978-0615708300
ISBN-10: 0615708307

CONTENTS

INTRODUCTION

One night I was sitting in an ORP quietly observing as rangers students gave incomplete instructions and never even bothered to see if they had been understood. They would never come back around and see if their tasks had been accomplished. A student who was not being graded asked others about the operation they were about to carry out. Some didn't know; a few seemed not to care. It bothered me that this one motivated soldier did not have a clue what he was supposed to do and those that offered what they knew conflicted with each other.

I thought to myself, 'This guy could be the next PL'. His squad leader came by and the uninformed ranger asked his questions again. "Don't worry about that" the squad leader replied, "We've got to get moving." I wondered what the squad leader would have done if he had known I was there. I also wondered why there was such a lack of leadership performance in the platoon and why it always seemed to be this way. They had sat through several leadership classes and were told exactly how they would be graded.

It was after this that I decided someone should put in print the do's and don'ts of Ranger School.

There needed to be something to tell the ranger candidate what was expected of him to pass a patrol and gives some insight to how the RI thinks. Why not me? I had several years of experience instructing and evaluating ranger students and I had worked in each of the phases.

So here it is. I didn't want to go into so much detail that it would be boring and loaded with unnecessary information. That could be why the Ranger Handbook is so rarely read. What I have done is explained the leadership tasks that are the basis for all grades, and then covered the phases of an average patrol. The things covered in this book are the ones that had better happen (or not happen, as it applies) for you to pass. I have not explained detailed techniques except in a few instances, but instead drawn the bottom line. If it's written in here then you can bet it should be remembered and applied.

Lastly, I would like to say that, while this book is directed at the ranger candidate, it could prove useful to anyone seeking to hone their leadership skills. Many of the 'stupid' things ranger students do, I have seen in TO&E units and the same leadership principals apply.

LEADERSHIP SKILLS

During your time in the chain of command your leadership skills will be evaluated. You will be given some basic patrolling training and evaluated on your ability to lead your unit in reconnaissance and combat missions. You don't have to be a tactical wizard to pass a patrol; you only have to display strong leadership. If you fail a patrol, it is probably not because you can't patrol, but because of your leadership abilities. Should this happen you need to ask yourself, "What caused me to fail and what leadership skills could have prevented it?" This is what it's all about and here I will tell you about the five areas of leadership that you will be evaluated on.

TAKE CHARGE

From the time you assume a leadership position, you have thirty minutes to complete the take charge process. This is not much time and there seems like enough things to do to take a few hours. The best way to get it done is by using your subordinate leaders. Don't do just one thing at a time. While there is no sequence to follow, I have used one here that should work well. First establish the priority of the tasks to be accomplished and delegate your authority to have subordinates get it done. For example, getting a complete and accurate status of your unit, informing the men of changes to the chain of command, and correcting unsatisfactory actions are things that can be done by sub-leaders while you exchange equipment and information with the previous leader and determine your location. Then immediately check security and the location and orientation of subordinate elements and crew served weapons. Get the status from your sub-leaders and ensure it is complete and accurate. Report your status to your higher and ensure that you know what your mission is. If needed, issue a FRAGO to your unit. This completes the take charge portion of your grade.

COMMUNICATION

The most unmotivated soldier is the one who is uninformed. The uninformed soldier is the one who does not know what to do on the OBJ and does whatever *he* thinks is right. This can be trouble. Your men will be more willing to bear hardships if you take the time to let them know why they are doing it. Passing back a pace count helps keep everyone informed and they feel more involved (and it doesn't take much effort on your part).

You are evaluated on how well you keep your subordinates informed, using the chain of command. When you give guidance to subordinate leaders, do so using specific instructions. Tell them exactly what you want them to do and how well it must be done. *Always* give them a time standard or they will assume there is none (give a mission statement). Use feedback to make sure that they understood your instructions the way you meant them. Having them repeat your instructions is one way to do it or you can just ask them, "Now, what are you going to do?"

When decisions need to be made, involve your subordinate leaders in the decision making process. You probably don't know everything and inviting suggestions invites communication. You have to establish a two-way flow of communication up as well as down the chain of command. Make yourself available to answer questions and *always* allow time for sub-leaders to disseminate information.

SUPERVISION

This is probably the most neglected of the leadership tasks. I have never failed a student who supervised well, because with proper supervision (along with good time management) everything gets done to standard.

Even though you know things will go your way if you do everything yourself, remember this: It Can't Be Done! You must use your subordinate leaders and when you do that, you have to supervise. Start by establishing priorities for everything that has to be done. Assign tasks to sub-leaders and tell them the priority. Use the chain of command and stay within your span of control (3 to 5 men). When you assign the tasks use good communication skills and issue specific instructions (task, condition, standard, when to start and when to be finished) and make sure they understand what you want done.

Let your subordinates do their jobs, don't try and do it for them. Check their progress from time to time to ensure the tasks are being accomplished. Make corrections when you find something wrong or progressing too slowly. Hold the sub-leaders responsible for the actions of their unit; *force* them to make their men meet the standard. You can fix a problem yourself, but it will just happen again if the man's immediate supervisor is not held accountable.

Supervision is not something that takes place only in the patrol base or during preparation for the mission, it is a constant process. You supervise during movement, enemy contact, actions on the OBJ, etc. You must always be at the most critical place to control your unit based on the mission and tactical situation. Maintaining a complete and accurate status of your men, equipment and sensitive items is also part of supervision. It helps you to plan and prioritize what needs to be done.

The most common error in supervision that I have observed is leaders walking around looking at deficiencies but not correcting them. For example, the PSG walks up from the rear of the platoon saying "Spread out!" then just lets his men blow him off. It is not enough to notice the problem; you MUST ensure it is corrected.

MOTIVATION

Double standards kill motivation. If your men are going to be motivated, you must set the example. Not just by acting motivated yourself, but by exceeding the standards in noise and light discipline, camouflage, keeping your ruck packed and so on.

You eat and sleep only after mission essential tasks are accomplished and the welfare of the men has been provided for. The smallest incident of not leading by example will cause you to fail motivation, if not your entire patrol.

Your attitude sets an example for your men too. If your attitude is less than positive, it will be noticed by your men. A poor attitude is contagious and can ruin your grade. Stamina is graded under motivation as well (both physical and mental). You must display the ability to think on your feet even on the last patrol of the FTX. This includes flexibility; things never go exactly as you would like them to especially when you are in contact with the enemy. Nonetheless someone has to make quick, sound decisions when your unit is caught in an ambush.

That should be the leader of that unit; and you will be graded on this under motivation.

Other things you must do include monitoring your men and providing rest halts, refilling canteens and rotating heavy equipment during movement. Ensure the rate of march is adjusted to suit the terrain and whatever it is that you are doing, ensure your subordinates work as a team. Finally, it is very important that you recognize those who perform well and encourage them to continue to do so.

INITIATIVE

During your graded patrol there will be numerous opportunities for you to demonstrate initiative. If you are the PL, don't ask the RI about every move you think you might make; this shows a lack of initiative. If you are the PSG or SL you must do what needs to be done in the absence of orders (like having claymores placed to cover the kill zone, even though no one told you to). When you are not given all necessary information – ask for it. And when someone higher in the chain of command is planning to do something stupid, you must make *forceful* recommendations of better courses of action.

PLANNING

When you receive a mission you will have to establish and maintain a secure area for planning. Don't just establish it and assume that your sub-leaders are maintaining it – remember to SUPERVISE. Get an up to date status report from your sub-leaders so that you can task organize your equipment and plan for maintenance and resupply. This will also help you to task organize your sub elements based on the number of men currently assigned to each one. This is very important; you cannot give an effective warning order without an accurate status.

Analyze your mission and determine exactly what it is that you have to do and then task organize your men, weapons, and equipment based on your METT-T analysis. When making your time schedule don't make the common mistake of taking the time up yourself. You will be graded on how much time you allow for sub-leaders to plan, disseminate, inspect and rehearse. You should make your time schedule realistic and then enforce it.

Assign specific tasks for subordinates to accomplish in preparation for the mission and OPORD (using specific instructions). For example, "F.O., we have five target numbers. Select the five best target locations in our AO and prepare a fire support overlay and target list. I want the major intersection north of the OBJ as a target. This is our general route. Brief me here in 20 minutes."

You must issue your warning order within 30 minutes of receiving your mission. All sub-leaders must be present at a minimum. Afterward you should conduct coordination; fire support as a minimum. If the order you got from higher says that another unit is operating close by, you need to coordinate with them. This is almost never done and units will travel the same way and bump into each other. It is bad when first platoon is ambushed and second platoon is 300m away and does not help because of lack of coordination. Never forget the RI's have probably been where you are going and may be able to give you detailed information about your OBJ; but only if you ask.

All leaders need to assist in the mission analysis and contribute to the plan. They also need to supervise preparations. Too often all of the leaders will huddle in the center of the perimeter and discuss the plan and never check on things such as security, routes, paragraph 5, the terrain model, sketches, etc. During the OPORD is not a good time to realize that TRPs were not planned to cover the alternate route; or the terrain model doesn't accurately reflect the OBJ. And the ORP is certainly not the place to find out that you don't have batteries for your NODs.

OPORD/FRAGO

Your order does not need to take forever. Put it out, ensure that it was understood, and allow time for it to be disseminated. Inspections may still be needed and you will need time to rehearse.

The following is the latest Ranger Course Operation Order format:

Time zone used throughout the order: If the operation will take place in one time zone, use that time zone throughout the order. If the operation spans several time zones, use Zulu time.

Task organization: How you have organized the unit for this operation,

1. SITUATION.

a. Area of Interest. Describe the area of interest or areas outside of your area of operation that can influence your area of operation.

b. Area of Operations. Describe the area of operations. Refer to the appropriate map and use overlays as needed.

(1) Terrain: Using the OAKOC format, state how the terrain will affect both friendly and enemy forces in the AO. Use the OAKOC from higher OPORD; but, refine it based on your analysis of the terrain in the AO.

(2) Weather. Describe the aspects of weather that impact operations. Consider the five military aspects of weather to drive your analysis (V, W, T, C, P - Visibility, Winds, Temperature/Humidity, Cloud Cover, Precipitation). Note the effects on enemy and friendly.

High Temp	Moon Rise	Sunrise
Low Temp	Moon Set	Sunset
Wind Speed	Moon Phase	BMNT
Wind Direction	% Illumination	EENT

c. Enemy Forces: (You can use what you received in the order from higher, but you need to give YOUR estimate of the enemy's probably course of action in your area as it pertains to your unit).

(1) State the enemy's composition, disposition, and strength.

(2) Describe his recent activities.

(3) Describe his known or suspected locations and capabilities.

(4) Describe the enemy's most likely and most dangerous course of action.

d. Friendly Forces: Information for this paragraph can be found in the higher headquarters' OPORD in paragraphs 1d, 2, and 3.

(1) Mission of next higher unit to include higher leader's intent

(a) Higher Headquarters Two Levels Up

1 Mission

2 Intent

(b) Higher Headquarters One Level Up

1 Mission

2 Intent

(2) Mission of Adjacent Units. State the locations of units to the left, right, front, and rear. State those units' tasks and purposes; and say how those units will influence yours,

particularly adjacent unit patrols (Include information obtained from adjacent unit coordination).

Left:

Right:

Front:

Rear:

2. **MISSION.**

Who, What (task), When, Where, and Why (purpose). The operation (raid, ambush, etc.) may be stated for clarity, but the task (interdict, destroy, etc.) must be included.

• State the mission clearly and concisely. Read it twice.
• Go to map and point out the exact location of the OBJ and the unit's present location.

3. EXECUTION.

a. Commander's Intent. The stated vision that defines the purpose of the operation. A concise statement of what the force must do and the conditions the force must establish with respect to the enemy, terrain, and civil considerations that represent the desired end state. This is an expansion of paragraph 2 and is not required at battalion level and below.

b. Concept of Operations. Write a clear, concise concept statement. Describe how the unit will accomplish its mission from start to finish. Base the number of subparagraphs, if any, on what the leader considers appropriate, the level of leadership, and the complexity of the operation. The following subparagraphs from FM 5-0 show what might be required within the concept of the operation. Ensure that you state the purpose of the war fighting functions within the concept of the operation.

WARFIGHTING FUNCTIONS
Fire support
Movement and Maneuver
Protection
Command and Control
Intelligence
Sustainment (formerly called "CSS")

c. Scheme of Movement and Maneuver.
Describe the employment of maneuver units in accordance with the concept of operations. Address subordinate units and attachments by name. State each one's mission as a task and purpose. Ensure that the subordinate units' missions support that of the main effort. Focus on actions on the objective. Include a detailed plan and criteria for engagement / disengagement, an alternate plan in case of compromise or unplanned enemy force movement, and a withdrawal plan. The brief is to be sequential, taking you from start to finish, covering all aspects of the operation.

- Brief from the start of your operation, to mission complete.
- Cover all routes, primary and alternate, from insertion to link-up, until mission complete.
- Brief your plan for crossing known danger areas.
- Brief your plan for reacting to enemy contact.
- Brief any approved targets/CCPs as you brief your routes.

d. Scheme of Fires.
State the scheme of fires to support the overall concept and state who (which maneuver unit) has priority of fire. Refer to the target list worksheet and overlay here, if applicable. Discuss specific targets and point them out on the terrain model

e. Casualty Evacuation. Provide a detailed CASEVAC plan during each phase of the operation. Include CCP locations, tentative extraction points, and methods of extraction.

f. Tasks to Subordinate Units. Clearly state the missions or tasks for each subordinate unit that reports directly to the headquarters issuing the order. List the units in the task organization, including reserves. Use a separate subparagraph for each subordinate unit. State only the tasks needed for comprehension, clarity, and emphasis. Place tactical tasks that affect two or more units in Coordinating Instructions (subparagraph 3h). Platoon leaders may task their subordinate squads to provide any of the following special teams: reconnaissance and security, assault, support, aid and litter, EPW and search, clearing, and demolitions. You may also include detailed instructions for the platoon sergeant, RTO, compass-man, and pace-man.

g. [*sic*] (subparagraph omitted in original)

h. Coordinating Instructions. This is always the last subparagraph under paragraph 3. List only the instructions that apply to two or more units, and which are not covered in unit SOPs. Use an annex for more complex instructions. The information listed below is required.

(1) Time Schedule. State the time, place, uniform, and priority of rehearsals, backbriefs, inspections, and movement.

(2) Commander's Critical Information Requirements. Include PIR and FFIR

(a) Priority intelligence requirements. PIR includes all intelligence that the commander must have for planning and decision making.

(b) Friendly force information requirements. FFIR include what the commander needs to know about friendly forces available for the operation. It can include personnel status, ammunition status, and leadership capabilities.

(3) Essential elements of friendly information. EEFI are critical aspects of friendly operations that, if known by the enemy, would compromise, lead to failure, or limit success of the operation.

(4) Risk-Reduction Control Measures. These are measures unique to the operation. They supplement the unit SOP and can include mission-oriented protective posture, operational exposure guidance, vehicle

recognition signals, and fratricide prevention measures.

(5) Rules of Engagement (ROE).

(6) Environmental Considerations.

(7) Force Protection.

4. SUSTAINMENT.

Describe the concept of sustainment to include logistics, personnel, and medical.

a. Logistics.

(1) Sustainment Overlay. Include current and proposed company trains locations, CCPs (include marking method), equipment collection points, HLZs, AXPs, and any friendly sustainment locations (FOBs, COPs etc.).

(2) Maintenance. Include weapons and equipment DX time and location.

(3) Transportation. State method and mode of transportation for infil/exfil, load plan, number of lifts/serials, bump plan, recovery assets, recovery plan.

(4) Supply.

Class I--Rations plan.

Class III--Petroleum.

Class V--Ammunition.

Class VII--Major end items.

Class VIII--Medical.

Class IX--Repair parts.

Distribution Methods.

(5) Field Services. Include any services provided or required (laundry, showers etc.).

b. Personnel Services Support.

(1) Method of marking and handling EPWs.

(2) Religious Services.

c. Army Health System Support.

(1) Medical Command and Control. Include location of medics; identify medical leadership, personnel controlling medics, and method of marking patients.

(2) Medical Treatment. State how wounded or injured Soldiers will be treated (self-aid, buddy aid, CLS, EMT etc.).

(3) Medical Evacuation. Describe how dead or wounded, friendly and enemy personnel will be evacuated and identify aid and litter teams. Include special equipment needed for evacuation.

(4) Preventive Medicine. Identify any preventive medicine Soldiers may need for the mission (sun block, Chap Stick, insect repellant, in-country specific medicine).

5. COMMAND AND CONTROL.

State where command and control facilities and key leaders are located during the operation.

a. Command.

(1) Location of Commander/Patrol Leader. State where the commander intends to be during the operation, by phase if the operation is phased.

(2) Succession of Command. State the succession of command if not covered in the unit's SOP.

b. Control.

(1) Command Posts. Describe the employment of command posts (CPs), including the location of each CP and its time of opening and closing, as appropriate. Typically at platoon level the only reference to command posts will be the company CP.

(2) Reports. List reports not covered in SOPs.

c. Signal. Describe the concept of signal support, including current SOI edition or refer to higher OPORD.

(1) Identify the SOI index that is in effect

(2) Identify methods of communication by priority

(3) Describe pyrotechnics and signals, to include arm and hand signals (demonstrate)

(4) Give code words such as OPSKEDs

(5) Give challenge and password (use behind friendly lines)

(6) Give number combination (use forward of friendly lines)

(7) Give running password

(8) Give recognition signals (near/ far and day/ night)

NOTE: Each plan in your order *must* be detailed and *specific* as it relates to the mission of your unit! Too often a student will explain a technique for the operation instead of giving a plan. For example, "I will leave the PSG a five point, take the squad leaders and conduct a leader's recon, emplace security, then support, and then assault. I will initiate a claymore and the signal to lift fires is a white star. We will gather the PIR and return to the ORP." This IS NOT A PLAN! It is however, the cause a lot of No-Go's for planning. Be specific and give the details of *how* you want to get each of these things done.

INSPECTIONS

Although inspecting is a continuous process for leaders, there are required inspections for planning. The initial inspection should be conducted as soon as you receive your mission. Check to see that all weapons and equipment are present and functioning properly and make a list of all deficiencies that you find. The initial inspection may be delegated to subordinate leaders to accomplish, but you should spot check their work.

The final inspection should be conducted after giving your subordinates time to correct all deficiencies, but not just before move-out. Use the list that was made earlier to ensure that corrections have been made. Use this opportunity to ask questions of the men to see that they understand the plan. The final inspection should be completed early enough to make corrections in case there are still deficiencies.

REHEARSALS

Rehearsals are critical to the success of any operation, but particularly when the operation will be conducted by a group with little experience of working together. Regardless of what everyone else does, you must ensure that your unit conducts rehearsals.

In garrison you will coordinate for a time and place for your rehearsals. Be there on time. There is no excuse for not conducting a full force rehearsal of actions on the OBJ.

When planning in the patrol base, you should use reduced force rehearsals. There are a number of ways to do this for example; the special teams can rehearse routine actions even before the order is issued. Squads can rotate from security to the terrain model to use brief backs. Just don't be the student who says he will conduct brief backs (to check the block) during the FRAGO and then never makes it happen.

Observe what happens during rehearsals; this is a good way to detect flaws in your plan. Get feedback from subordinates and make necessary changes. This is the time to find and correct deficiencies not during actions on the OBJ. Remember that your efforts while rehearsing may be wasted if you don't ensure changes to the original plan are passed on to everyone.

MOVEMENT

One of the key areas of your movement grade is your ability to navigate. All leaders must remain oriented to within 200 meters. Do this by studying the map before you move and staying alert during movement. Don't wait until an RI says, "Ranger, show me where you are on the map." to figure it out. I can assure you that will not reflect well on you.

Follow the route that was planned. You can change it if you need to, but make sure the change gets disseminated to everyone. Enforce proper movement formations and techniques for your unit. Yes, you can change these as needed too, but use common sense and enforce your orders. Moving up a steep hill or through a nasty marsh, does not make the "ranger file" the best formation to use. Your buddies will want to move however it's easiest for them, but if you say traveling overwatch and wedge, then make them do it – it's your grade.

Each leader should move at a place within his unit where he can control it best. You are responsible for maintaining accountability of your men, enforcing security, noise and light discipline and ensuring that they relay all signals (i.e. rally points), be where you can do this. If signals, head counts, etc. are not getting passed to everyone, find the problem and fix it. A way to do this is to send a signal and then follow it; you will be able to find who it is that's not passing it on.

At halts, immediately check the positioning of your men and machine gun(s). Everyone must make the best use of available cover and concealment and have a sector of fire. Leaders at all levels should spot check this as first priority. Ensure everyone is aware five minutes before restarting movement, this aids motivation and helps prevent breaks in contact.

Cross or bypass danger areas IAW the plan. There are a number of techniques you can use, but there are a few things to remember. The job of flank security is to provide the main body with early warning; they can hardly do this when their position is 20 feet from the crossing point. No matter how many times students get chewed out for doing this, the next chain of command seems to think they can get away with it. *It always counts against you.*

Don't sit right next to a danger area to decide how to cross, and don't stay there long (I will never understand why people think this is a good place for a map check). Maintain control and accountability and get away from danger areas quickly. Most RI's will give you more problems to worry about if you are screwing this up (indirect fire, ambush, casualties, etc.).

The purpose of all movement is to get your unit from one place to another so that you can execute some task. As the leader, you must get your men there, with their equipment, in time to accomplish the mission.

RECONNAISSANCE PATROLS

These tend to be your easier missions because they are usually conducted by squads and don't involve contact with the enemy, making control easier. You will be graded on area recons as squads or zone recons as a platoon. Either way, you will usually end up having squads conducting area recons.

If you are the platoon leader tasked with a zone reconnaissance, select one of the recon techniques described in the Ranger Handbook and issue your plan (see ORP under Combat Patrols). From there it is up to the squad leaders to gather the PIR, and you should let him do it his way (IAW your plan). You are still responsible for selecting OBJs for each squad and ensuring the recons are completed on time. Control squads during the recon by having them report check points, phase lines, etc. You must also control link up, whether it's at the platoon ORP or a rendezvous point. When the platoon has completed link up and all PIR has been gathered, disseminate all information to the platoon and notify higher headquarters.

If you are the squad leader conducting an area reconnaissance, you will have to give a detailed order to your squad to cover actions one you leave the platoon. Emplace a surveillance team during your leaders' recon after identifying the OBJ.

Disseminate any changes to the plan to everyone and ensure that R&S teams take the necessary equipment (NODs, BINOs, etc.).

Ensure that everything is done in a controlled manner, to include departure of the ORP and link up and this should be an easy GO. A squad leader grade as part of a platoon operation would be easier to pass if students would keep the same aggressive attitude as they do when they are in charge of an independent squad.

One of the things that make this an easy grade is the lack of control problems. If you make contact with the enemy, you may lose this advantage. Likewise, if you blow off danger areas and so forth, the RI may take some action that will make control more difficult for you.

COMBAT PATROLS

Although the Ranger Course is beginning to transition to more squad missions, the majority of the operations you will be evaluated on are still the ambush and raid. Both are very similar in execution so I will explain the combat patrol in three phases and call attention to the differences between the raid and ambush when necessary.

OBJECTIVE RALLY POINT

Occupying the ORP and occupying the patrol base are almost exactly the same; therefore, this action is done at least twice a day. This is the one task that you do more than any other. That's why it's hard to understand why some students take two hours to do it. This wasted time could be used on the leaders' recon (a task that is too often 'finger drilled'). You should spend no more than 45 minutes occupying the ORP.

A squad can recon their ORP by just moving around the area or occupy by force. This is generally not accepted for a platoon. The requirement is that you establish a security halt about 200 meters from the tentative ORP and assemble the recon team. Ensure that there are enough men on the recon team to provide security at the ORP and for the PL on the way back to the platoon. If there are enough radios available, the recon team should have two; one to leave at the ORP and one to remain with the PL. The PL must give a contingency plan to the PSG and it must be disseminated to the entire platoon. The recon party will select and secure an ORP based on METT-T (a common mistake is putting it too close to the OBJ).

When the recon element departs, the fire team leaders should report to the PSG to get instructions for assisting in adjustment of the perimeter and dissemination of the contingency plan. After this is done they should put the platoon in an order of movement that will make occupying the ORP easiest. This will be based on your SOP for occupation.

Without an understood SOP, control will be difficult during occupation of the ORP. Be alert for problems and quick to make corrections when you notice one. When positioning men, make the best use of available cover and concealment and each of them should be assigned a sector of fire. Don't let your men cluster together or stand around and make sure that they are in the prone, observing their sector of fire once they are in position. No one should be allowed to talk, dig around in their rucksack, or turn on a flashlight (100% alert!)

LEADERS RECONNAISSANCE

Once the ORP is established, quickly begin preparations for the leaders' recon. Everyone going to recon the OBJ should begin to reapply camouflage and get their special equipment ready while the rest of the platoon provides security. All squad leaders should be going on the recon and therefore, must leave instructions to their senior team leaders about tasks to accomplish during the recon.

The PSG must assemble the recon element in a controlled manner and inspect them to ensure they have all necessary equipment. This is best accomplished by inspecting a couple of them at a time and then positioning them outside of the perimeter. When the recon element is ready the PSG informs the PL and receives the contingency plan.

The recon element must be especially cautious while moving forward of the ORP. I have seen many patrols turn ugly by having the leaders make contact with the enemy while separated from the main body. This will cause severe control problems, not to mention that a ranger student surprised this way tends to take the wrong action, if any at all. Use your binoculars or NODs and don't get any closer to your OBJ than you have to.

Your first action upon making eye contact with the OBJ should be to emplace a surveillance tam, leaving everyone else (except a few men for security) in the release point. This team should have a clear view of the entire OBJ and a radio at a minimum. You will be doing yourself a favor if you have one of these men draw a sketch of the OBJ and the surrounding terrain. You can use this to brief any changes to the plan.

The PL must recon each elements position with that element leader. The route from the release point to each position should be reconnoitered to ensure that it is concealed from the OBJ. If it is not, the alternate route should be checked on the way back. There are characteristics that each position should have and things that must be designated.

Security Positions – You do not have to physically go to these positions. A map recon is enough if you are short on time and if you ensure that the leaders of the security teams know where you want them. The positions should have cover and concealment, good fields of fire, and a natural obstacle between them and the avenue of approach. If a natural obstacle is not there, use a claymore. You should try to put some terrain between the security teams and the OBJ to protect them from fires. If there is no terrain suitable for this, be careful not to have these positions in someone's sector of fire. RIs check closely to see if your placement of personnel would cause fratricide (and grade you accordingly). One last consideration for your security positions is their distance from the OBJ. You need to think about the enemy's capabilities and put the security teams far enough out to accomplish their missions (initially to give you early warning). If the enemy was driving toward your main body at 30 MPH and the security position was 400m out, you could have as little as 15 seconds before the enemy was on you.

Support Position – Your support position needs to be as far away from the OBJ as you can put it while staying within the effective range of your weapons. It should have cover and concealment, good fields of fire, and enough room to space your machine guns 10-15 meters apart. Don't assume that because you can see the OBJ that your gunners will be able to hit it. Get on the ground and look from that level (the RI probably will). The PL should designate the primary sector for engaging the OBJ, to include assigning the priority of targets, and the sector to be covered after the guns shift fires. The WSL should do the same for each weapon in this element. Take care not to include any friendly positions in these sectors. The standard clearly states no casualties from "friendly" fire and it is left up to the instructor to determine whether or not it happens.

Assault Position – Select a position that is large enough to accommodate your assault element with about five meters between men. It should also have cover, concealment and fields of fire onto your OBJ. Your assault position must be far enough from the

OBJ that you will not alert the enemy during occupation, but close enough to assault if you should become compromised. The PL should assign sectors to squad leaders and state the priority of targets. Squad leaders must break this sector and priority down as it relates to their teams and weapons.

Take the leaders' recon seriously and don't waste your time by just going up there to "check the block". A lot of students will look around only long enough to pinpoint the OBJ, and then go back to the ORP without designating positions. The only thing this accomplishes is knowing how to find the OBJ. Even if you may be late, it ain't worth doing if it ain't worth doing right.

PREPARATIONS IN THE ORP

After the recon party departs, the PSG must use the senior team leaders to adjust the perimeter and disseminate instructions to support the contingency plan (the PSG may need to organize a reaction team that was not planned for earlier). When this is accomplished security should be maintained at 100% until the PL determines that the ORP is no longer tentative.

Communications must be kept with the PL during the recon. Once the PSG gets the word from the PL, he should begin final preparations for actions on the OBJ. Everyone should reapply camouflage, and obtain their mission essential equipment (this may involve getting items from others and you should have a plan for distributing radios, NODs, etc.) All equipment must be ready to work prior to leaving the ORP. Battery operated items should be turned on and allowed to "warm up", LAWs should be extended, lubricate weapons, and test everything before departing.

It is a good idea to organize rucksacks in a way, so that when you return, you don't have to wait on someone who cannot find his ruck. Grouping them as a fire team is one way or you may prefer to line them up by squads. Leaving individual rucks lying around is asking for trouble.

The platoon should be ready for actions on the OBJ when the recon element returns. The last thing to do is put the men into a movement formation. They should be in the order that they will occupy the OBJ and in a cigar-shaped perimeter.

When the leaders return to the ORP, they have to brief their men on what they found on the OBJ and any changes to the plan. Squad leaders should check to ensure their instructions were carried out by the team leaders and the men have their special equipment.

ACTIONS ON THE OBJECTIVE

The PL must leave a contingency plan with ORP security and wait for all other security elements to report in position before occupation. Leaders must control departure from the ORP and movement to the release point. Take care to move stealthily.

Prior to releasing the support element the PL should check with surveillance to ensure that nothing has changed on the OBJ. The assault element will wait silently while support occupies their position. The WSL should set in his gunners and then explain to each of them their sectors of fire and the priority of fires within each sector (an RI will check the positioning of the guns and ask gunners about how they are to engage the OBJ – this can be a key factor in the WSLs grade). When all gunners have been briefed, the WSL must report to the PL that the support element is in position.

NOTE: A technique is to have the PSG in charge of the support element, but this takes a key leader away from the place where the most leadership is needed. A variation is to have the PSG with support initially and have him follow the assault element to the OBJ.

The assault element is the most likely to lose control. This is normally the largest element to move to and occupy the OBJ. I have seen RIs make up their minds about a student's grade when the leaders have a 'pow-wow' while the assault element gathers around like cattle. One cause of this is just indecisiveness; another is conducting a poor leaders' recon and then trying to give a FRAGO during occupation. The bottom line here is that occupation (by all elements) must be done in an orderly manner.

Squad leaders should move their men into position and issue sectors of fire, the priority of targets, and assault lanes to the team leaders. Allow the team leaders to issue instructions in support of this and check what they put out and how the men are oriented and report to the PL.

At some point the PL will need to bring in the surveillance team (unless the assault element formed around them). They can be used as guides at the release point, local security or integrated into assault element.

AMBUSH SPECIFICS

After the assault element is in position, they will need to emplace claymores to cover the entire kill zone (another task that is commonly finger drilled). Afterward the PL and PSG should go through and check the positioning of elements and men, and then wait for the target to arrive.

Initiation of the ambush is a key decision by itself. You don't want to initiate just because there is someone in your kill zone. The flank security teams must report the identification, size of element, speed, and direction of travel to the PL who must make the decision whether or not to initiate.

The PL should give at least two initiation signals at the same time. For example, tell the WSL "FIRE" at the same time you fire the claymores. If you let the enemy pass through your kill zone, (and this happens usually because everyone is asleep) everything else you do will be for "training benefit". You will surely fail.

Whether or not to assault the kill zone should be based on the purpose given in the OPORD from higher. If you can satisfy the commander's intent without sending the assault element across the kill zone, then don't send them. This is really common sense but a lot of students assault just to do it. The advantage in not crossing the kill zone (or sending only minimum personnel) is avoiding control problems. For example, if you need to gather PIR, you can have most of the platoon overwatch while the search teams go to the kill zone and do their jobs. You may want to send a fire team with them to provide added security. In this case you have only a handful of men to control making things run a lot more smoothly.

If you feel you need to assault the kill zone, do so following the guidelines in the next section. From this point on, the ambush is conducted the same as the raid. I will explain raid specifics and then pick back up on the common events under the heading Consolidate and Reorganize.

RAID SPECIFICS

When all of your elements are in position you are ready to initiate. It should go without saying that you must initiate with your most casualty producing weapon; but every now and then there is a student who plans to use a whistle or flare. A PL who does this is almost certainly a NoGo, but going down with him will be the PSG and squad leaders because they let it happen. Initiation is most often done by signaling the support element over the radio, but sometimes radios fail and therefore you should have a contingency.

The best thing to do is when you release the support element to occupy their position, tell the WSL what time to initiate. For example, "It should take you about 30 minutes to set your men in; the assault element will need about 20 minutes. If you don't hear from me in one hour, go ahead and initiate." The only thing that can screw this up is if the assault element is not in position when support starts to fire.

Once the WSL gets the signal to fire, he must immediately relay it to his gunners. He must then supervise the engagement of the OBJ and not let the assault element be hit by his fires. Don't be the WSL who is sitting back letting the guns make noise when an RI walks in from the rear of your position. "Actions on the OBJ" is one of the most important parts of your grade and you should be totally involved in the actions of your men. Another common mistake made by a WSL is not to take corrective action when a gun malfunctions. Several times I have actually witnessed the WSL crouch beside a gunner to observe his actions and when the gun jammed, get up and move to another gun. The thing to do here is to get the gun back up first.

As the support element gains fire superiority over the enemy, the assault element should quietly move closer to the OBJ until one of the three things happen: (1) You run out of cover/concealment, (2) You come upon the limits of the enemy's defensive position (or an obstacle), or (3) You get too close to the fires of your support element. At this time you should give the signal to assault and have the support element shift its fires. The signal should not be given by yelling, but by a weapon firing. The idea here is not to let the enemy know where your main assault is coming from until you are engaging them. Too often the position of the assault element is given away as soon as the support begins to fire. It happens when people start yelling to direct movement instead of using hand and arm signals and leadership by example.

Once the assault begins, all leaders involved must ensure that it is controlled. Don't allow part of the element to get out ahead of everyone else. When this happens, they tend to mask the fires of those to the rear and RI's may assess friendly fire casualties (and on top of that being detrimental to your grade, it also makes more work for you to handle the casualties). As long as you are receiving fire, everyone should make maximum use of cover, concealment, and IMT. If you are not being fired upon, just get everyone quickly across the OBJ.

While crossing the OBJ all enemy personnel should be disarmed and any vehicles, bunkers, or buildings should be cleared. No one should spray a thin skinned vehicle or building with automatic fire. Doing so will most always result in friendly casualties being assessed. Just cautiously look inside and if there is enemy there, fire just enough well-aimed shots to eliminate the threat.

CONSOLIDATE AND REORGANIZE

Upon reaching the far side of the OBJ, the PL and squad leaders should immediately establish security and prepare for a counter attack. Sectors of fire must be issued and positions must be mutually supporting. Everyone should load a full magazine into their weapon, and team leaders must get a status of their men. Before anything else is done ACE reports must be submitted by all elements. The chain of command must be reestablished to include replacing key leaders and personnel. Redistribute ammunition (within and between squads) and identify casualties.

While a hasty perimeter is being established, the PSG should be checking the OBJ and establishing a priority for the actions he will supervise (search teams, aid & litter, etc.) He needs to tell the PL what special team(s) he wants first. When the PL has security taken care of, he sends the teams to the PSG. It is up to the PL and squad leaders to continue to adjust the perimeter and not let it get spread too thin. It is essential to control that the special teams go directly to the PSG for instructions and return to their squad leader only when directed.

When the PSG gets control of the special teams he must issue them specific instructions. The search teams will need to know which areas to search and the priority of search, where to consolidate the PIR or prisoners and they should be reminded to return directly to the PSG when they complete their tasks. The aid & litter teams will need to know where the wounded are and what the priority of treatment is. Use the medic to help supervise casualty evacuation. The PSG must keep track of who he sends to carry casualties to the collection point (or ORP as you designate).

The PSG must actively supervise the actions of the special teams and ensure they get the job done as quickly as possible. Search teams especially take an excessive amount of time by doing things like checking for PIR inside enemy boots and measuring the tread wear on tires. Be realistic. You will be given a list of PIR; that is what you should look for.

As the special teams complete their tasks, the PSG must check to ensure his instructions were carried out and then send the men back to their squad leaders. The squad leaders must continue to work with each other and the PL, adjusting the perimeter as men come and go.

WITHDRAWAL

Once you have accomplished your mission you should quickly depart from the area of the OBJ. Your withdrawal must be controlled and not an every man for himself dash to the ORP. You can have an SOP for withdrawal and adjust it in the order to fit each particular OBJ. The key thing to remember is to provide overwatch as elements withdraw and to maintain accountability for all men and equipment. Each element should withdraw to the same place they were released from (ORP or release point) and must do so in reverse order of occupation.

Back at the ORP you must pass out rucks and move out quickly. Remember that noise and light discipline is important departing the OBJ just as it was moving in. When you have moved a safe distance away, stop and consolidate information and sketches and then allow time for this to be disseminated to everyone.

PATROL BASE

Your platoon will normally operate a patrol base at least twice a day. Some grades will be little more than occupation and operation of a patrol base; therefore, you could pass or fail based solely on your actions here.

OCCUPATION

Occupation of the patrol base can be done by the same technique you use for the ORP. It does not matter how you set your men in to the perimeter as long as you keep control. Don't allow the men to cluster around; and enforce noise and light discipline. The key thing is to set up a secure perimeter as quickly and quietly as possible without losing control.

The difference between occupying an ORP and a patrol base is that with a patrol base you have LP/OP's and R&S teams. A temporary LP/OP must be established to watch your trail during occupation. This should be about a three man team and they should have a radio, NODs (if at night), and a claymore at a minimum.

Once the platoon has initially occupied, you must send R&S teams to recon the area around your site. The PL should gather the squad leaders and tell them what to have the teams look for. Generally they must look for any signs of enemy activity, avenues of approach, dead space, and a source of water. The PL must be specific about what he wants each team to do based on their sector. For example, you may give each team checkpoints to ensure certain areas are checked and you may want one of them to look for a certain known point so you can confirm you location. The teams must be given a time to depart and a 'time window' in which to return. You should give a mission statement and your briefing should follow the FRAGO format.

The squad leaders must give the briefing to their R&S teams and ensure they have the necessary equipment (they must have a radio if you have enough). Before the R&S teams can depart, everyone in the platoon must know they are leaving. This is the case anytime someone leaves the patrol base or whenever someone is returning.

The routes of the R&S teams must be coordinated to avoid having them accidentally run into one another. One way to do this is to have them depart on the left side of their squads sector and return on the right. They should recon the entire sector out to 400 to 600 meters in the day time. At night however, there is the greater chance they could become lost and cause you major hassles. An approved technique to use at night is to send them out from the center of their sector on azimuth for 200 to 300 meters, conduct a listening halt and return.

While the R&S teams are gone, the perimeter must be 100 percent alert. The PL should use this time to come up with an alternate patrol base and two rendezvous points (evacuation plan) if it was not given in the FRAGO. When the teams come back, if the PL decides to use this area for the patrol base, the evacuation plan will be ready to issue.

As the R&S teams return they must be debriefed and you will use this information to decide whether or not to move and how to adjust the perimeter if you stay. Remember, no planning or work priority can start until after the final adjustment of the perimeter.

It's best to emplace the permanent LP/OP(s) first so that you don't have to readjust the perimeter again after they leave. You must maintain at least one LP/OP while you are in the patrol base. Your LP/OPS must be placed where they can observe the most likely avenue to your position and should be able to watch dead space. They must have (1) communications with the platoon CP (preferably wire) and (2) a detailed contingency plan.

Everyone must be briefed about the location of the LP/OP. The PSG should initially emplace them so that he knows where they are, when it is time to replace them. You should see that they are rotated about every hour (put this on your time schedule). They must not eat, sleep, or perform maintenance at the LP/OP. It is a good idea to inspect them before taking them out to ensure they are not taking chow, poncho liners, etc. Some students try to be everyone's buddy and allow LP/OPs and other such security tasks to be "get over" jobs and even encourage such behavior. But when one of your men is caught eating, sleeping, etc. when they shouldn't be, it's your grade that suffers.

Make sure that your machine guns are oriented to cover the most likely enemy avenues of approach. They should have as much grazing fire as possible and if the gunner can only see 50 meters to his front, *Move Him!* About the quickest thing you can do to fail is to have a machine gun aimed into a tree or brush pile. Yes, you should try to pick the best positions the first time, but if you need to readjust, it's better for you to do it on your own than to be told later, "Ranger, I've already took note of it, but you need to move this gun, he can't see how to fire it through this tree". If there is no real avenue of approach to worry about you can just have the guns cover across the front of their squads.

Check the entire perimeter and make sure there is at least ten meters between positions. Everyone should be making the best use of available cover and concealment. No one should be able to shoot the LP/OPs. Make any corrections and determine where claymores should be emplaced and you can begin making your sector sketch. This should all be done and final before you dig your position in. Yes, in the latter phases you must dig it in.

Squad leaders must prepare their sector sketches and turn a copy in to the PL, who will compile the platoon sketch. You must take care to make your sketches as accurate as possible (azimuths must be properly oriented and you should scale it as well as you can). The squad sketch must depict: magnetic north, each position and the type of weapons there, sectors for each position, machine gun FPLs or PDF, dead space, claymores, major terrain features, and the location of LP/OPs.

The PL must spot check the squad sketches for accuracy before making his sketch. The platoon sketch must include: magnetic north, squad sectors, machine gun positions and their sectors, claymores, planned indirect fires, LP/OP locations, and the CP.

The platoon sector sketch is an illustration of your fire plan. To complete occupation of the patrol base, your men must know your alert and evacuation plans. These can be SOP but the evacuation plan must include the specific location of your rendezvous points and alternate patrol base.

The RIs will check your occupation by looking at how you emplaced your men and weapons on the perimeter and where you put your LP/OPs. Usually they will conduct their own debriefing of the R&S teams and use this information along with their knowledge of the terrain to question your site selection and positioning of men and weapons. They will compare your sector sketch with the actual perimeter looking for discrepancies. They will ask questions of the men on the line to see if the plans have been disseminated. It's not a bad idea to have everyone write down the location of the LP/OPS, alternate patrol base and rendezvous points. If they can't remember, this shows that they were told.

PRIORITIES OF WORK

Once you have completed occupation, you can jump into your priority of work. You must have a plan for this and it must be based upon the condition of the patrol. Don't assume that you don't need to conduct weapons maintenance just because they have not been fired all day. The previous maintenance may have been substandard. If you think you will skip this task, you had better conduct a good spot check before you make the decision. The order in which you have the priorities is up to you but you must be able to justify it to the RI.

Work priorities can be accomplished by two different techniques. One way is to allow the squad leaders to start the next task when they have finished the first. The other way is to have the entire platoon finish a task before anyone moves on the next one. I recommend the second technique because it is easier to control. In a TO&E unit I would not use this method, but in Ranger School it helps because you can easily see if someone is doing something they shouldn't be and quickly make the correction.

Whichever method you decide to use, no one can be allowed to start the next task until the first one has been checked. A common mistake is putting the tasks on a time schedule and letting the squads move from task to task at the proper time. This leads to poor maintenance and men waiting around until it's time to eat and sleep. You should conduct priority of work by briefing the squad leaders one task at a time. Give them a task, condition and standard including a time to start and a time to be finished and then check their progress from time to time. When everyone has met the standard, move on to the next task. Be sure that when you give the task you are specific about what you want done. Don't give them a choice. I have heard many times things like "Okay, now we are going to do personal hygiene. Have them shave, and then if they want, they can change socks". If you think you need to change socks, then that's it, they change their socks; and if you think they need to sleep, they sleep. If you give your men an option, then it's not that big of a *priority* is it?

Briefing the squad leaders before each task is the best way to keep them from getting ahead of you. You may think that as long as it gets done quickly it doesn't matter how they do it. What matters is whether or not you are controlling your men and inspecting to ensure standards are met. You cannot maintain this control if everyone is doing their own thing.

You cannot get your weapons cleaned in half an hour. Most students allow about this much time anyway so they can get on to the next task. Here is a plan that will get all weapons and equipment maintained in two hours (that will normally leave you with plenty of time for chow, sleep, etc.) In this example gun team 1 is with first squad, and so forth. When a gun is being cleaned the squad they are attached to is at 100 percent alert.

Have gun team 1 work on their gun (1st sqd 100%) while guns 2 and 3 are alert. Second and third squads maintain their rifles keeping one man alert per position. Allow 40 minutes for this – 40 minutes down for cleaning (2nd sqd 100%) while first squad works on their rifles. Third squad has already finished their rifles and can't break down their M60 (no more than one gun down at a time); so they have 40 minutes to work on radios, NODs, etc. Then while gun 3 is down, first and second squads can maintain their equipment. This will take two hours, give or take, based on how well the time is used.

Before talking about hygiene let me just say that camouflage does not fall into this category as a priority of work. Camouflage is a security measure. You should take the time to apply camouflage whenever you need to. Yes, you will need to after you shave, but that doesn't excuse you from running around without it in the meantime. You should allow about 30 minutes for hygiene (depending on what you want done) and no more than that for chow. So you should be able to have all of these tasks accomplished within three hours and use the rest of your time to get some sleep. Of course it won't be quite this simple if you have to plan because there will be a few other tasks to get accomplished.

There are a few things that you need to pay attention to while conducting these priorities of work. Don't let your men have excess equipment out of their rucksacks. You have to be prepared to evacuate the patrol base on a moment's notice and no matter what he tells you, your ranger buddy can't pack all of that stuff away while en route to the alternate patrol base.

There are a lot of good reasons why he has the shaving kit, LAW, batteries and maps scattered on the ground around his ruck, but there is no excuse. If it appears to the instructors that you are operating a gypsy camp, you will get to practice your evacuation plan. Unsecured equipment always seems to get the attention of the enemy. ☺

Don't let your men do their work priorities at their positions. Have them pull back about ten meters off the perimeter and use the available cover or at least concealment. Another important point here is that everyone must complete the work priorities. The leaders must set the example. When an instructor checks maintenance, the most common places to find discrepancies are with the RTOs, LP/OP and the leaders themselves. You must rotate duties in order for everyone to get their work done. You can plan so that the LP/OP is from the squad that is 100% alert, and the RTOs can swap out, but the leaders will have to make time and be efficient.

OTHER CONSIDERATIONS

There are other tasks that may need to be accomplished such as water resupply or a team may need to be sent to handle resupply of food or ammo. In the mountains it may be necessary to send a team to high ground to send reports to higher. Whenever you dispatch an element from your patrol base, you must give them a contingency plan and ensure that they have sufficient security and communications. The entire platoon must be informed before the element departs and should be periodically reminded that there is a friendly element outside of the perimeter.

I have already covered how to use R&S teams at night, but there are a few other things that must be considered if you occupy in the dark. Maintenance is difficult in darkness and there is a good chance that small parts will become lost. Only disassemble weapons that are inoperative. Other weapons may still be cleaned, but don't break them down farther than the bolt. Due to depth perception being different at night (and some people not wanting to be alone), your perimeter will usually be smaller when occupied after darkness. This will need to be corrected after stand-to. When you prepare your sector sketch, the only things you can accurately include are the positions and sectors. You will have to wait until after stand-to to complete it.

I waited until now to talk about the rest plan because it is not something you will do every day unless you are really on top of things (and so is everyone else). There's not much to it except that you must make sure to maintain security and noise and light discipline. Do this by having a separate rest plan for leaders. The PL, PSG, or WSL should be up, as well as one rifle squad leader, all of the time. Remember when you *check* the perimeter, you must make corrections.

Stand-to must be conducted in the morning and evening in the patrol base. It should begin prior to BMNT/EENT and last until after the sun rises or sets. Everything must be packed and ready to move and everyone must be in their positions and alert. For a night patrol base when things are going against you, this can be a last chance to excel or a nail in the coffin. Many instructors will look around at stand-to and make a final decision on someone who performed marginally. Sleeping Rangers, chow and poncho liners lying around are not going to tip the scales in your favor.

NON-GRADED POSITIONS

There are several positions that you may be assigned to that do not count as a patrol. Such positions as RTO, fire team leader, FO, and medic are all opportunities for you to earn a plus spot report. In addition to earning a spot report, you have the opportunity to improve your peer grade. Because these positions allow you to work directly with those who are being graded, if you perform well they will probably remember it when they fill out your peer report.

You can not only make points with your peers, but also with the instructors. If you put all your efforts into the performance of these jobs, the instructors will very likely pass the word on to the next group of RI's. If you have acquired a reputation as always being a team leader, RTO, etc. and doing your best to help everyone pass, you are more likely to get a GO than the guy who keeps a low profile.

There is still another advantage to performing these tasks. If you are one of these key individuals in the patrol, you will usually know a lot more about what's going on than the average rifleman. This is a big plus if you happen to suddenly find yourself in charge.

SPOT REPORTS

Spot reports are used to record the performance of students who are not in a graded position. They range from real good (major plus) to real bad (major minus). A major spot is equal to three minor spots. A major minus cancels out three minor plus'. If you accumulate three major minus spots in any one phase of the course, or five in total you are considered for recycle. If you accumulate eight major minus spots throughout the course you will be dropped.

Here are some examples of how spots are issued.

Negative Spot Reports

Minor minus:

- Improper uniform or equipment for training.

- Dirty weapon.

- Administrative chain of command not working.

- Equipment not secured.

- Loss of minor item of equipment.

- Sleeping at a time when not scheduled - 1st time.

- Violation of noise or light discipline - 1st time.

- Breaking contact – less than 30 minutes.

- Late less than a minute.

- Fail to DX unserviceable equipment

- Fail to negotiate an obstacle – confidence course.

Major minus:

- Fail˙ to follow instructions by RI or student leaders.

- Weapon Dirty or rusty – does not function properly.

- Sleeping in a tactical situation.

- Violation of noise or light discipline - 2nd time.

• Breaking contact – 30 minutes or more.

• Accidental discharge.

• Weapon not loaded in a tactical situation.

• Safety violations.

• Not supporting the chain of command.

• Falling out of any run.

• Weapon not under positive control.

• Having contraband.

Positive Spot Reports

Minor plus:

- Excellent terrain model, sketches, etc.

- Outstanding performance as squad member.

- Outstanding performance in non-graded position.

Major plus:

- Superior performance in administrative chain of command for a complete phase.

- Superior performance in a non-graded position.

- Max land navigation or the knot test

RANGER STUDENT ETIQUETTE

Last, but certainly not least, I need to make sure you know how to interact with the instructors. Well, I *shouldn't need to*, but there has been the occasional student who opens his mouth and lets all changes of passing a patrol drift off like so much hot air. You must always treat the RI with proper respect and military courtesy. Never give him any "lip" whatsoever. Don't make any facial gestures when talking with an RI. Most instructors are approachable and eager to help you or answer your questions; just don't get on the bad side of one. Keep in mind that the RI, and his buddies, can give you what you came for *or* make it that much more difficult for you.

On the other hand, don't try to "kiss up" to an RI. It's very easy to tell when someone keeps coming around trying to get on your good side. This is much more common, but irritating to the instructor. This type of behavior could get you labeled a "spot lighter" and draw extra attention to you when you are being graded.

<u>CONCLUSION</u>

No, it's not the whole course in concentrated form, but it is the most important parts. What we have covered here is what really matters if you want to earn the tab. Take this book as good advice. I know there are the things the RI's want to see; I've worked with them long enough to know. Remember, it's the leadership tasks that get you there. The other things are just there as a way to evaluate that leadership.

Get on the mailing list for book updates, additional resources, and other info at rangerschoolprep.com

RANGERS LEAD THE WAY!

27379066R00041

Made in the USA
Lexington, KY
07 November 2013